PUTTING THE PLANET FIRST

REDUCING, REUSING, AND RECYCLING WASTE

REBECCA RISSMAN

CRABTREE
PUBLISHING COMPANY
WWW.CRABTREEBOOKS.COM

CRABTREE
PUBLISHING COMPANY
WWW.CRABTREEBOOKS.COM

Published in Canada
Crabtree Publishing
616 Welland Avenue
St. Catharines, ON
L2M 5V6

Published in the United States
Crabtree Publishing
PMB 59051
350 Fifth Ave, 59th Floor
New York, NY 10118

Published in 2019 by Crabtree Publishing Company

Printed in the U.S.A./082018/CG20180601

Author: Rebecca Rissman

Editorial director: Kathy Middleton

Editors: Paul Mason, Elizabeth Brent, Ellen Rodger

Proofreader: Lorna Notsch

Interior design: Peter Clayman

Prepress technician: Ken Wright

Print coordinator: Katherine Berti

Images:
All images courtesy of Shutterstock except pages P7: Getty Images/ Zing Images; p13: Getty Images/Christian Science Monitor; p15: Getty Images/Thony Belizaire; p19: oconnelll/Shutterstock.com; p21: Getty Images/Arpad Benedek; p27: Getty Images/Tony Robins.

Every attempt has been made to clear copyright. Should there be any inadvertent omission, please apply to the publisher for rectification.

The website addresses (URLs) included in this book were valid at the time of going to press. However, it is possible that contents or addresses may have changed since the publication of this book. No responsibility for any such changes can be accepted by either the author or the Publisher.

Library and Archives Canada Cataloguing in Publication

Rissman, Rebecca, author
        Reducing, reusing, and recycling waste / Rebecca Rissman.

(Putting the planet first)
Includes index.
Issued in print and electronic formats.
ISBN 978-0-7787-5031-4 (hardcover).--
ISBN 978-0-7787-5035-2 (softcover).--
ISBN 978-1-4271-2144-8 (HTML)

        1. Waste minimization--Juvenile literature. 2. Refuse and refuse disposal--Juvenile literature. 3. Recycling (Waste, etc.)--Juvenile literature. I. Title.

TD793.9.R57 2018   j363.72'82   C2018-902463-1
                                                                C2018-902464-X

Library of Congress Cataloging-in-Publication Data

Names: Rissman, Rebecca, author.
Title: Reducing, reusing, and recycling waste / Rebecca Rissman.
Description: New York, New York : Crabtree Publishing Company, 2019. |
    Series: Putting the planet first | Includes index. |
Identifiers: LCCN 2018021421 (print) | LCCN 2018026371 (ebook) |
    ISBN 9781427121448 (Electronic) |
    ISBN 9780778750314 (hardcover) |
    ISBN 9780778750352 (paperback)
Subjects: LCSH: Recycling (Waste, etc.)--Juvenile literature.
Classification: LCC TD794.5 (ebook) | LCC TD794.5 .R617 2019 (print) |
    DDC 628.4/458--dc23
LC record available at https://lccn.loc.gov/2018021421

CONTENTS

EARTH IN TROUBLE – HELP NEEDED!

Garbage litters the ground, smog **hangs in the air, and giant islands of plastic waste float in the sea. Earth's environment is in trouble. But it's not too late. You can help!**

You have probably already heard about **pollution**. It is the name for harmful substances in the environment. Some of Earth's air, water, and land is polluted. Much of this pollution comes from human activity, such as driving cars and operating large factories.

POLLUTION AND GLOBAL WARMING

Our pollution contributes to global warming – the increase in Earth's average temperature. As the planet gets warmer, it is affecting our weather and climate. There has been an increase in droughts, and more extreme weather. Global warming is changing Earth's **ecosystem**.

COLLECTED FROM BEACHES IN 2015

| 1,024,470 PLASTIC BOTTLES | 888,589 FOOD PACKAGES | 861,340 PLASTIC BOTTLE CAPS | 827,056 PLASTIC BAGS | 439,571 PLASTIC STRAWS |

In 2015, volunteers picked up garbage from beaches around the world. They kept track of what they found. Many of the items they collected could have been recycled.

Trash washed up on a beach in Vietnam

FIGHTING GLOBAL WARMING

People can fight global warming by reducing pollution. Because making things causes pollution, making fewer new goods will help. Reusing old items, reducing the number of new things you buy, and recycling as much as you can are all ways to do this. These simple steps can be very helpful and can reverse some of the harm done to Earth's environment. They can also help to prevent new problems caused by pollution.

TOO MUCH GARBAGE

People create a lot of waste. They throw away old food, plastic, paper, metal, glass, and much more. The amount of waste we create is causing problems around the world.

Garbage is bulky, smelly, and sometimes dangerous until it can **degrade**. Once it degrades, garbage can become part of the soil again. Some garbage – for example, batteries – contains harmful substances. So garbage that is not safely contained can pollute the **habitats** of living things.

Some garbage degrades quickly. Items such as apple cores and used tissues break down in a few weeks. Other items take a very long time to degrade. A glass bottle can take up to one million years to break down. Some items even become **toxic** while they are degrading, such as certain plastics that release dangerous chemicals over time.

WHAT'S IN THE CAN?

Much of the world's garbage is made up of things that could be recycled.

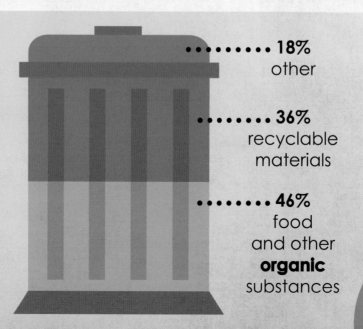

•••••••••• **18%** other

•••••••• **36%** recyclable materials

•••••••• **46%** food and other **organic** substances

6

Employees responsible for throwing away their own trash are often better at recycling it.

TINY GARBAGE PAILS

Many people don't think about how much rubbish they throw away. In the U.S. and Canada, though, a simple idea is changing things. Office workers are given tiny, individual garbage pails for their desks. They are also each given larger boxes for their recycling.

When an employee's garbage pail or recycling box is full, they must empty it. The tiny garbage pail fills up quickly. The larger recycling bin takes longer to fill. This makes people think about how much waste they produce and encourages them to recycle more of their garbage.

This idea has helped offices to greatly reduce their waste and has increased the amount they recycle.

REDUCING OUR GARBAGE

How can you help with Earth's garbage problem? Simple—just reduce your garbage! There are lots of ways to reduce the amount of waste we create.

USING REUSABLES

Reusable items, such as metal water bottles, cloth shopping bags, or ceramic coffee mugs help the environment. These items can be used over and over again, which reduces the number of **disposable** items that are thrown away.

Another way to reduce waste is to avoid buying products with a lot of packaging. Plastic bags, cardboard boxes, and metal tins are all types of packaging. Making packaging causes pollution, so buying items that have more packaging than necessary is wasteful.

THE MAGIC MUG

1 reusable mug can save ...

=

... 22.9 pounds (10.4 kg) of waste and ...

+

... 500 paper cups ...

... in just one year!

OLD FASHION IS THE NEW FASHION

Buying and selling at thrift shops and pre-owned clothing stores, such as Value Village, is a great way to reduce waste. People don't have to throw away clothing that is in good condition but no longer fits them. They can give or sell it to the thrift shop instead. While they are there, they can also buy vintage clothing, which is fashion from an earlier period in time.

As well as reducing waste, buying pre-owned clothing reduces the amount of new clothing that people buy. If you buy a pre-owned coat, for example, you don't need to buy a brand new one.

Finally, pre-owned clothing stores reduce packaging, because the clothing does not need new tags, bags, or plastic hangers.

REUSING OLD ITEMS

You probably already reuse things every day without even noticing. A water glass, breakfast bowl, and brush are all items you use over and over again.

Reusing objects doesn't only reduce the amount of waste people throw out. It also means new items need not be produced, packaged, and sold. This saves energy and money, as well as waste.

Some items can be used many times for the same purpose, like a glass or a toothbrush. Other things can be reused in new ways. Sometimes, an old item can even be reused in a way that actually increases its value. For example, an old coin can be made into part of a necklace. This is called **upcycling**.

Old items do not have to be used in the same way again. Sometimes it is fun to find a new use for them.

THE MANY USES FOR A JAM JAR

PENCIL HOLDER

FLOWER VASE

JAM JAR

SPICE JAR

SNOW GLOBE

THE PLASTIC-BAG FEE

Supermarkets in the U.S. and Canada used to give away billions of free plastic bags for shoppers to carry groceries in. These bags were often used only once and then thrown away.

Many cities have now passed laws that supermarkets must charge shoppers for each plastic bag they use. This encourages people to use their own reusable bags.

These new laws have been very effective. In less than one year, many supermarkets reduced their plastic-bag use by 80 percent.

Laws like this have also been passed in other countries. They have reduced the number of plastic bags littering the landscape and in **landfills**.

Plastic bags get caught in trees and litter the landscape.

RECYCLE AS MUCH AS POSSIBLE

Recycling—using the materials from old products to make new ones—is fast, easy, and cheap, and it has many benefits.

RECYCLING ADVANTAGES

Recycling reduces pollution: It takes less energy and materials to make a recycled product than a new one from scratch. It also costs less money to create goods using recycled materials. This means that in addition to helping the environment, recycling helps businesses and individuals save time and money.

RECYCLING FAILS

Despite the benefits, most countries recycle less than 50 percent of their waste. So why aren't more people recycling? Some say that they do not understand which materials are recyclable, others forget to do it, and still others think that it is too much work.

TIN-CAN POWER

Recycling 1 tin can ...

... saves enough energy for ...

... 3 hours of TV.

TRASH-FREE TOWN

The Japanese city of Kamikatsu used to burn its garbage. But city leaders knew this was harming the environment, so they decided to change the way the city dealt with its waste.

Kamikatsu started a very strict recycling program. People there must sort their garbage into 34 different categories. They also donate items they don't want anymore to a community shop. Other residents can come to this shop and pick things up at no cost.

Sorting garbage into different categories helps Kamikatsu to recycle waste more efficiently.

Today, Kamikatsu recycles, reuses, and **composts** about 80 percent of its waste. The remaining 20 percent goes into landfills. The city hopes to create zero waste by the year 2020.

NASTY PLASTIC

Plastics are nearly everywhere you look. You might even be sitting on a plastic chair right now! Plastics are very useful, but they are also harming Earth's environment.

PLASTIC PLANET

Although plastic is recyclable, most plastic waste is thrown away, and does not **biodegrade**. Instead, it breaks down into small pieces that end up in Earth's water supply, being eaten by animals, and even in our food. Even worse, these tiny bits of plastic often contain harmful chemicals.

THE GREAT PACIFIC GARBAGE PATCH

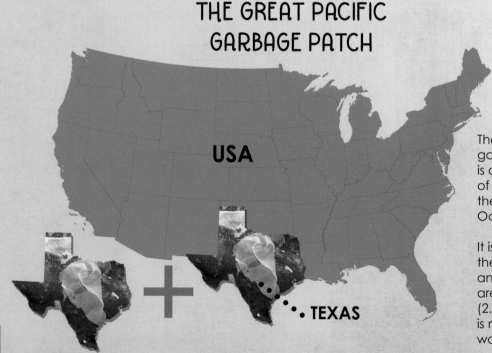

USA

TEXAS

Pacific Ocean

The Pacific garbage patch is a huge area of trash floating in the North Pacific Ocean.

It is about twice the size of Texas, and in some areas is 8.8 feet (2.7 m) deep. It is mostly plastic waste.

Companies such as Thread are providing job opportunities and helping the environment at the same time!

THE MAGIC OF RECYCLED PLASTIC

The Caribbean country of Haiti has a problem with plastic pollution. It also has a problem with unemployment – many Haitians cannot find work.

An American company called Thread decided to solve both problems at once. Thread hires people in Haiti to collect plastic trash, which is then washed, shredded, and turned into plastic threads. These threads are used to make fabric for clothing, shoes, and bags.

More and more companies are joining this eco-friendly trend. Fabric made from recycled plastic is so soft, you'd never know it came from a shredded plastic bottle. Clothing made from recycled materials usually has a tag telling you about its origins.

PAPER PROBLEMS

Paper products are easy to recycle. In fact, a single sheet of paper can be recycled up to seven times! Yet wastepaper clogs our waterways and spills out of landfills.

THE COST OF PAPER

Making new paper – instead of recycling – contributes to **deforestation**, pollutes the environment, and is also expensive.

New paper products are made from trees. Cutting down the trees, turning the wood into pulp for paper, and then cutting, printing, and packaging the paper uses a lot of energy. In some countries, paper mills have been responsible for releasing harmful pollution into rivers.

PAPER TREES

A single tree can produce a lot of paper products.

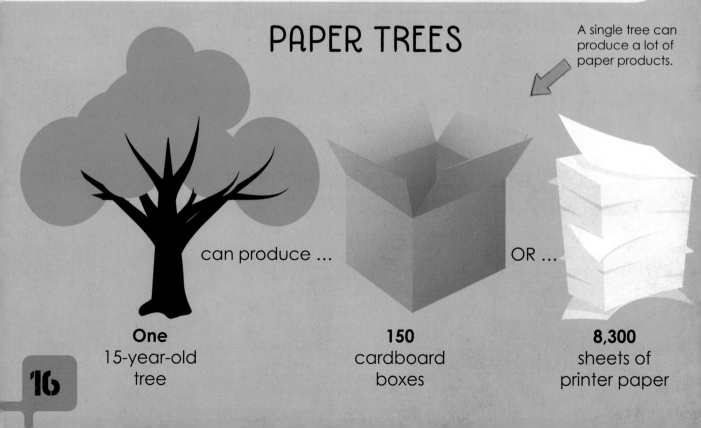

can produce ...   OR ...

One
15-year-old
tree

150
cardboard
boxes

8,300
sheets of
printer paper

PAPERLESS SCHOOLS

Going digital makes sense for many schools since students are usually very familiar with digital technology.

One school in Scotland knew it was using too much paper, so administrators decided to do something drastic.

They went digital, scrapped their paper and pen routines, and gave each student a tablet. Teachers were given laptops.

Instead of taking notes on paper, students take notes on their tablets. Teachers have stopped using paper handouts and started e-mailing them instead.

This digital revolution has been a huge success. It is popular with students and teachers, and the school has saved money on paper and printing.

WASTED METAL

Next time you take a sip from an aluminum can, ask yourself how many times it has been recycled. The answer might surprise you. Aluminium, like many other metals, such as copper and steel, can be recycled an infinite **number of times!**

RUBBISH METAL

Despite being highly recyclable, metal still shows up in garbage dumps and landfills. Each day, millions of metal food and drink cans are dumped in landfills. Most of these cans are recyclable.

People sometimes say that they have trouble understanding which metal items can be recycled. Learning more about what can and cannot be recycled is a great way to help the environment.

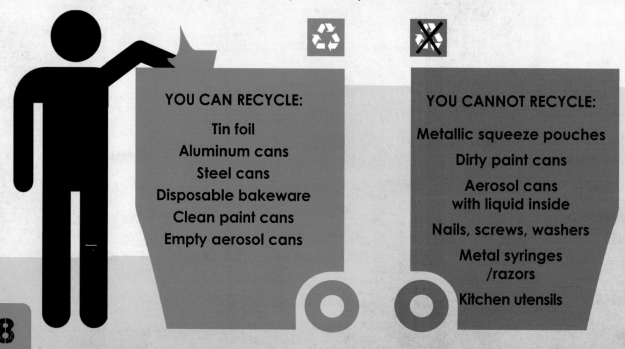

YOU CAN RECYCLE:

Tin foil
Aluminum cans
Steel cans
Disposable bakeware
Clean paint cans
Empty aerosol cans

YOU CANNOT RECYCLE:

Metallic squeeze pouches

Dirty paint cans

Aerosol cans
with liquid inside

Nails, screws, washers

Metal syringes
/razors

Kitchen utensils

METAL CHALLENGE

The Aluminium Challenge is a yearly contest in the United Kingdom. It asks students to come up with creative uses for aluminum in three categories: transportation, packaging, and construction. Students from around the world submit their designs and compete to see who can come up with the most creative, innovative ideas. Winners go to a celebration dinner.

The winners of the 2015 transportation category designed an eco-friendly car. It is powered by batteries and **solar panels**. If the battery runs out, the team designed a pedal under the front seat that can be used to recharge the battery.

With a bit of creative thinking, recycling can transform all sorts of things!

CANNED FACTS

$1 billion dollars worth of aluminum cans is thrown away each year in the U.S.

67 percent of aluminum cans are recycled in the U.S.

Recycling aluminum saves energy. It is the most valuable item in the recycling bin.

GLASS IN THE BIN

Toss your used glass jar into the recycling bin and mark your calendar. In just one month's time, that jar may have been recycled into a completely new product!

Families in the U.K. use about 500 glass jars and bottles every year. When glass containers are thrown away, they become a problem for the environment. Glass does not degrade, or break down, so it takes up space in dumps and landfills. Broken glass can also be dangerous if not disposed of carefully.

Making fresh glass from old jars and bottles uses less energy and materials than starting from scratch. In fact, the energy saved from making one bottle out of recycled glass is enough to power a computer for 30 minutes!

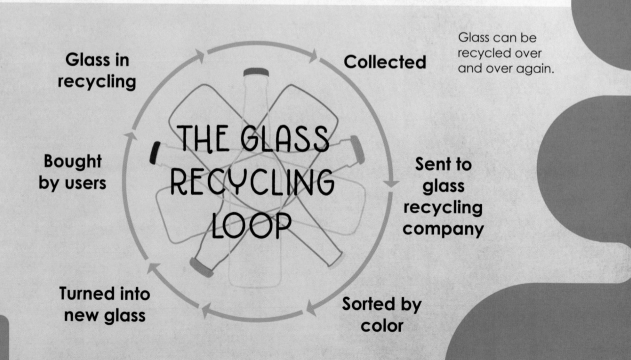

Glass in recycling

Collected

Glass can be recycled over and over again.

Bought by users

THE GLASS RECYCLING LOOP

Sent to glass recycling company

Turned into new glass

Sorted by color

These glass bottles add beautiful light and color to buildings.

BUILDING FROM THE BIN

Most builders use materials such as wood, stone, and brick to construct a new home. But a few **innovators** are getting their building supplies from an unusual place: the recycling bin!

Around the world, creative builders are using glass bottles, aluminium cans, old tires, and even plastic to build their homes. Some of these buildings are created to raise awareness or as public art pieces. Others are used as real-life homes.

Tito Ingenieri, a builder in Brazil, has become famous for his unusual home. He built it from more than six million glass bottles he found in his local garbage dump.

FOOD SCRAPS

Food waste is one of the biggest reasons for Earth's waste problem. Food waste decays slowly when it is buried under other garbage in a landfill. This contributes to the problem of pollution and overflowing landfills.

Hotel buffets are lavish and can sometimes be wasteful.

Food is wasted for many different reasons. Stores often stock too much of a certain type of food. If not enough customers buy it, the store throws it out when it gets too old. Restaurants often serve large portions of food. If a diner doesn't finish his or her plate, the leftovers are thrown away.

Food waste does not have to be a problem for the environment. When food waste is composted, it can turn into healthy and rich soil, which can be used to grow plants. However, few people compost their food waste.

WASTED FOOD

Each week in the U.S. ...

... half of all produce is tossed in the trash, but one in seven Americans use **food banks** (46.7 million people in 2015).

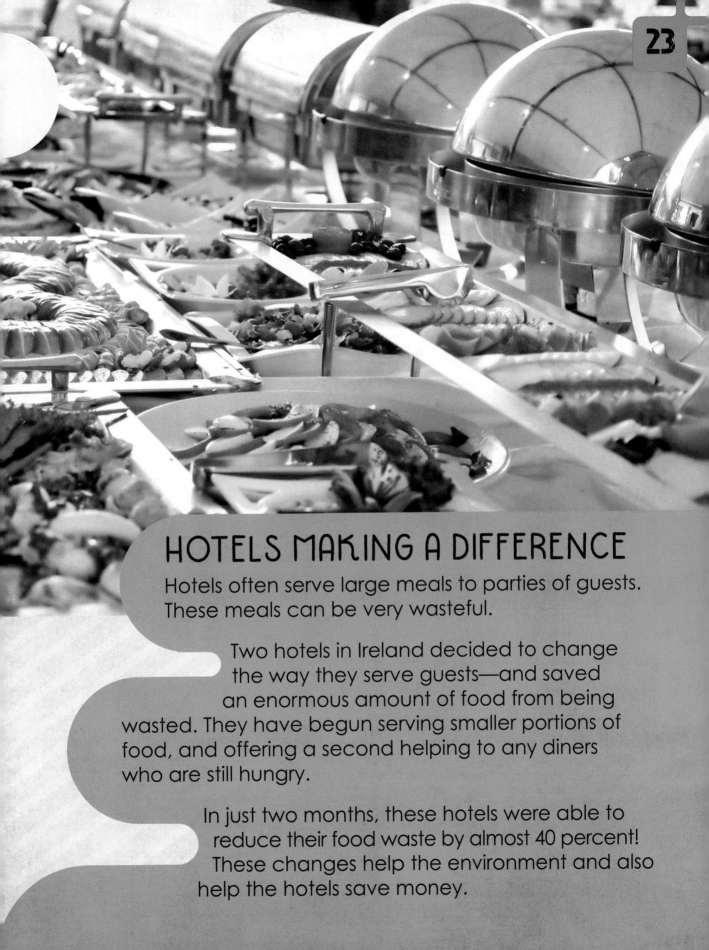

HOTELS MAKING A DIFFERENCE

Hotels often serve large meals to parties of guests. These meals can be very wasteful.

Two hotels in Ireland decided to change the way they serve guests—and saved an enormous amount of food from being wasted. They have begun serving smaller portions of food, and offering a second helping to any diners who are still hungry.

In just two months, these hotels were able to reduce their food waste by almost 40 percent! These changes help the environment and also help the hotels save money.

E-WASTE

What happens to your old TV when you get a new one? How about your mobile phone or computer? A lot of these items end up in landfills, contributing to Earth's pollution problem.

E-WASTE

E-waste is the name for electronic goods that are thrown away. Electronics are often replaced after only a few years, which means more and more are getting tossed into the trash. Dealing with e-waste is a growing problem

Electronics are often small and difficult to break down, and they sometimes contain toxic substances. Some recycling businesses buy e-waste, break it down, and resell the **components** that can be recycled or reused. However, this process is difficult and slow. This is one reason why much of the world's e-waste still ends up in landfills.

E-WASTE IN THE BIN, 2014

For every piece of e-waste that is recycled ...

... five pieces are thrown away

Old mobile phones that still work can be reused by people in need.

CANADA CALLING

Some organizations work to increase e-waste recycling. In Canada, the Canadian Wireless Telecommunications Association (CWTA) has created a national program called Recycle My Cell to make recycling old mobile phones easy.

People can go to the program's website recyclemycell.ca to look for a place in their city to drop off old phones and accessories. If there is not a location that is nearby, you can click on a link to print out a pre-paid shipping label to send the phone by mail. Donated phones are wiped of their information, and are reused or recycled for parts within Canada.

The CWTA has recycled more than 7.5 million devices since 2005.

WORKING TOGETHER

If you recycled all of your paper waste for a week, could you fill a whole bin? Maybe – but if your whole class worked together, you definitely could! We can do more when we work together.

Earth's waste problems can seem overwhelming. But when communities work together to reduce, reuse, and recycle, they can fight some of the problems caused by waste and pollution.

Countries in the European Union, for example, have set a goal to recycle at least 65 percent of all garbage by 2030. They expect to do this by enforcing new rules about separating garbage for recycling, making it illegal to put biodegradable waste into landfills, and charging fees for waste collection. Around the world, other countries and organizations have similar aims.

RECYCLING ON THE RISE

In the United States, people have been recycling more and more each year.

2005
79.8 million tons
(72.4 million metric tons)

2008
85.2 million tons
(77.3 million metric tons)

2013
87.1 million tons
(79.1 million metric tons)

Restaurants that serve food in reusable containers help the environment.

OPERATION ZERO WASTE

Tamsin Chen wanted to change the world, so the 19-year-old from Singapore started Operation Zero Waste Dabao.

Dabao means takeout in Cantonese. Chen had seen how wasteful takeout food packaging could be. She knew most people used the plastic food containers only once before throwing them away. She understood this was harming the environment.

Chen challenged food vendors to change. She asked them to reduce the amount of plastic packaging they used on a local holiday called National Day. She encouraged people to bring their own containers for food on this day. Operation Zero Waste was a great success. It managed to reduce the amount of plastic waste thrown away on National Day by 75 percent.

Chen hopes that people will continue to reduce their use of disposable takeout containers in the future.

THINKING OF THE FUTURE

When you think of the future, what comes to mind? Do you imagine flying cars or hologram voicemails? What about a pollution-free planet?

New technologies are evolving every day that make reducing waste and reusing and recycling materials easier than ever. These advances are coming from many different sources. Behind some of the best ideas is a massive range of people, from famous scientists to big companies and even children!

A company in India is making knives, forks, and spoons that are completely edible. When you're done with them, just chomp them down! Another company, in the U.S., is making carpeting from recycled materials. The carpet cleans the air by trapping **pollutants** in its **fibers**. New, environmentally friendly products like these are appearing every week.

BIODEGRADABLE VERSUS NON-BIODEGRADABLE FORKS

Corn-plastic forks degrade in **30 days**.

Sugarcane-plastic forks degrade in **45 days**.

Nonbiodegradable plastic forks degrade in about **100 years**. Biodegradable plastics, such as corn plastic and sugarcane plastic, break down and become harmless to the environment very quickly.

FAMOUS TRASH

In Northern California, a giant white building has become famous. But why? It's the Sacramento BioDigester—the biggest waste digester in North America.

Waste digesters turn food waste into electricity, heat, fuel, and other types of energy. Tiny organisms called **bacteria** break down the waste inside the biodigesters. They produce a gas called **methane**, which can be captured and turned into energy.

Biodigesters of all sizes are popping up in cities around the world.

The Sacramento BioDigester is a large, efficient energy machine. It converts nearly 100 tons (90.7 tonnes) of waste into energy each day.

GLOSSARY

bacteria Tiny organisms that can break down waste

biodegrade To be broken down by living organisms, such as bacteria

compost Rotted organic matter, added to soil for extra nutrients

component A part of something

deforestation Cutting down forest and not replanting it

degrade To break down

disposable Something intended to be used only once

ecosystem A community of living things that interact

fiber A fine, thread-like part of material or a carpet

food banks Organizations that collect food and distribute it to those who need it

habitat The natural home of a living thing

infinite Endless

innovator A person with new ideas or ways of doing things

landfill A large outdoor area where waste is piled and covered

methane A gas that is produced when some materials decay

organic Plants or animals raised without the use of pesticides, chemical fertilizers, or hormones

pollutant A substance that pollutes

pollution Harmful substances in the environment

smog A mixture of fog and pollutants

solar panel A flat panel that absorbs energy from the Sun's rays in order to generate electricity

toxic Poisonous

upcycle To reuse something in a way that increases its value

waterway A water-filled channel, such as a canal or river

FINDING OUT MORE

WEBSITES

Learn more about recycling at this helpful site:
www.epa.gov/recycle

The National Institute of Environmental Health Sciences has games and activities for young recyclers and environmentalists:
www.kids.niehs.nih.gov

Learn more about Kamikatsu here:
https://youtu.be/eym10GGidQU

FURTHER READING

Living in a Sustainable Way: Green Communities
by Megan Kopp (Crabtree, 2016).

Leaving Our Mark: Reducing Our Carbon Footprint
by Nancy Dickman (Crabtree, 2016).

Putting Earth First: Eating and Living Green
by Megan Kopp (Crabtree, 2016).

INDEX